UNDERSTANDING THE
HISTORY AND RECORDS
OF NONCONFORMITY

Patrick Palgrave-Moore BA, FSA, FSG

elvery
dowers

Printed in England by W.H. Hutchins & Sons, Norwich, Norfolk.

First Published 1987
2nd Edition 1988
Elvery Dowers Publications
13 West Parade, Norwich, Norfolk

LIST OF CONTENTS

Introduction

In presenting this booklet for the beginner and for the more experienced researcher into family history, I have attempted to show how a study of nonconformity may be of some benefit. Researchers are shown not only what records might be available but how these records could be viewed in the wider context of religious mobility. They are given a better opportunity of placing their research in its proper context, knowing where it might lead and what results might be expected. To some extent, this study provides the very material for 'clothing the skeleton'. Family historians today are ever conscious of placing their ancestors in a social environment, rather than assembling data purely by reference to names, places and dates. For those of our ancestors who left little record of their lives, there is perhaps a greater need to describe their environments, their pressures and their motivations in more detail.

I am only too aware of the rashness of trying to summarise the entire history of English religious development within a few pages and in doing so, will surely have omitted many important and relevant points. I have also tried to avoid turning this into an historical treatise as many learned works on the subject already abound. Nevertheless, a general understanding of the historical background to nonconformity is essential and I have purposely dealt at some length with this aspect in the first part of the booklet. Some bias against the Established Church will be evident. Again, this is intentional, but used merely to highlight the pressures against dissenting activity.

Finally, I readily acknowledge the enormous help provided principally by Don Steel's excellent definitive works on the subject, most of the dates from which I have been able to use in this booklet. I should also emphasize that I have taken the subject matter to embrace all Christian denominations outside the Church of England for a study of purely English nonconformity.

PART ONE – HISTORICAL BACKGROUND

Tudor Change

There is perhaps a view of early religious development in England that sees change in sudden events, no more so than at the time of the Reformation. This over-simplistic if not naive view denies that spirit of Englishness which generally abhorred change. The mediaeval Church had certainly become moribund and its lack of urgency in reform gave rise to protestations throughout Europe, expressed most popularly by such men as Luther and Calvin. It was not until the Counter Reformation of the sixteenth century that the Church put its own House in order, but delay had only served to foment dissent. This Protestant ethic of dissent found little favour in England, where Henry VIII viewed its principles as heretical and actively persecuted those who professed them. However, although this emerging dissent proved a useful tool in his divorce, leading to his break with Rome, Henry retained belief in Catholic doctrine until his death. His dissolution of the monasteries was partly a reform of the power of the Church but as much a political act which drew on anti-clerical feeling to replenish the Crown's coffers. The ascendancy of a small Protestant elite under his son Edward, continued the rape of the nation's heritage and introduced religious change. The influx of Protestant Dutch and Walloon workers into such centres as London, Norwich, Canterbury and Southampton widened further this religious dissent but there was no nationalistic movement in its favour. If anything, the country felt embittered. The rich had become richer but the poor remained poor.

Mary Tudor's abolition of these religious changes and their partial restoration under Elizabeth, left the humble parishioner more in a state of apathy. Elizabeth's wish for a new Protestant Church with Catholic ceremonial was perhaps a compromise which might have appealed to the English sense of independence. However the **Acts of Supremacy and Uniformity** in 1559, not only imposed these new practices but also denied religious freedom. On the one hand, Catholicism was made illegal, and on the other hand, the retention of Catholic ritual embittered those with extremist views. To many, the Acts were unacceptable. Several clergy were deprived of their livings but perhaps the greatest effect was felt by large numbers of clergy abandoning their livings rather than subscribe to the new Articles. Within a few years, East Anglia for example, normally regarded as a hotbed for dissent, had some 36% of its parishes without clergy, many of which by 1600 had fallen into permanent decay. However, in the main, where services were possible, the parishioner tended to follow his priest. Doctrinal changes had to come slowly following the mood of the country and there is reason to believe that for the first decade of Elizabeth's reign, church attendance at this Catholic form of service, continued much as before.

The growth of Dissent

Elizabeth's excommunication from Rome in 1570 tended to divide the nation further. Now, Catholics had to declare their allegience and faced crippling fines for refusing to attend the Protestant service. Hopes that a religion forced on the nation would at least eventually dispel opposition through lack of ministering clergy did not allow for Englishmen returning from abroad as Benedictine, Jesuit or Dominican priests. Imprisonment and forfeiture of estate for recusancy and often a cruel death for discovered Catholic clergy forced all but the wealthy few to give at least the outward signs of compliance, yet the Faith survived the penal years. At the same time a number of English clergy who wished to purify the Church from all Catholic practices, remained within the Church to press for even wider reform. Thomas Cartwright, who believed in the Calvinist principal of replacing Episcopacy by elected ministers, emerged as a leader of these purifiers or Puritans. Another body of clergy known as Separatists or Independents held the view that congregations and not membership by residence should determine the basis for a church and accordingly saw their position as being outside a national church. Robert Browne, whose followers became known as Brownists formed the first Congregational Meeting in Norwich as early as 1580, but they, and the rest of the Puritan movement at this time, were never strong, were often despised and the more extreme of them were executed. By 1593, effective persecution and restriction had virtually erased all form of Puritan activity from English life and its supporters moved to Holland.

By the time of James's accession in 1603, the English Church was weak. A State religion forced upon the nation was never likely to succeed. More than half of the clergy had received no formal training and even licensed preachers were ill-used and often reduced to poverty. The breeding ground for dissent was therefore well-placed. Catholics said perhaps optimistically to still number a million, looked to the Stuart line for a return to Rome or at least freedom of worship, whilst the Presbyterians hoped to forge closer links with their brethren in the Scottish Church. Neither faction fared well under the early Stuarts. The wealthier Catholics were fined heavily for recusancy and despite their growing strength in Parliament, Puritans who refused to accept church discipline were suppressed. In 1604, 300 Puritan clergy were ejected, setting a tone on future policy. To many, this prospect encouraged a new independent religious spirit. In 1609, John Smythe seceeded from the Amsterdam Church and formed a group of Baptists or Anabaptists, repudiating the Calvinist doctrine of pre-destination and restricting baptism to those old enough to believe. Their first meeting which was formed in London in 1611, became known as General Baptist. In 1616, the Independents formed a Congregation at Southwark. By 1631 they had ten more Congregations in London and by 1640, they had eighty. In 1633, a group of Calvinists left the Southwark group to form a Particular Baptist Congregation, retaining adult baptism but adopting pre-destination and independent church government. Although the Puritan movement expanded, under the reign of Charles I and particularly under Archbishop Laud, further growth was checked and openly suppressed.

The greater toleration of the Protectorate found favour with a renewed tide of anti-clerical feeling. Its sympathisers were strongest where recent economic change has gone furthest, notably in the towns, but even in rural areas the new mood was setting in. Whereas Laud had required uniformity, he had allowed variety in belief. The full Presbyterian system which Parliament now adopted was intolerant and rigourously required acceptance of dogma, morals and discipline, shifting opinion towards the Independents. Strongest among the army and the poor, the Independents formed more permanent new chapels at Yarmouth and Norwich in 1642. The General Baptists, strongest in the Eastern counties formed chapels at Portsmouth (1640), and Dover (1643) and by 1658 had some 155 chapels throughout the country. The most important new Particular Baptist Chapel was that formed at Taunton in 1647. Other groups, immune to the machinations of religious turmoil, found solace in a belief of personal religion without church, ministry or dogma. These were the Seekers, later known as the Friends or Quakers. In the time of George Fox who espoused their beliefs and developed an independent movement, their refusal to pay tithes or to take oaths and other idiosyncrasies, made the term 'Quaker' synonymous with abuse and ridicule. Nevertheless, despite heavy persecution during the Commonwealth and even after the Restoration, the movement grew rapidly from the east midlands in the 1640's through the north and south in the 1650's, often drawing upon members of the older denominations, particularly the Baptists.

The extremism of the Puritan movement, had, by the time of the Restoration in 1660, sickened the nation's taste for religion and a fee for a return to old values became widespread. For a generation to come Puritans were bitterly persecuted, none more so than the Quakers. The Act of Uniformity in 1662 required all ministers to be Episcopally ordained and to accept the Book of Common Prayer. As a result, almost two thousand ministers were ejected. The subsequent **Conventicle Act** of 1664 and the **Five Mile Act** of 1665, tried to ensure that there were no major re-groupings. A temporary respite came in 1672 with a **Declaration of Indulgence** giving relief to Catholic and Protestant Dissenters alike and under which, meetings and dissenting teachers could obtain licences. Of some 1609 licences granted to ministers three quarters related to those ejected in 1662. Presbyterians still hoped for a reformed national Church and their reluctance to accept independent status made their position somewhat nebulous. Certainly, the boundaries between them and the Congregationalists had become less marked and it is frequently difficult to determine which observances were being followed. Support for this toleration soon waned and the laws of suppression were re-imposed with equal severity. The **Test Act** of 1673, effectively debarred Catholic and Protestant Dissenters from civil or military office, though less so in the case of the latter. The so-called 'Clarendon Code' also stamped down on the dissenters, by now, mainly middle and lower classes, drawn from the ranks of merchants and artisans in the Cities and the industrial districts.

The accession of a Catholic Monarch in 1685 brought renewed hope to the Catholic minority. Catholic chapels appeared throughout the country and some form of national organisation returned. James planned initially to extend toleration to all Dissenters and even welcomed further imigration from persecuted French Protestants. Some forty thousand Huguenots are said to have settled in England, chiefly in the towns and in the ports and comprising chiefly artisans but with a number of the nobility and the peasantry. In his anger at the lack of support for this toleration, James opened the gates of office to Catholics on a wide scale, a move which was swift enough to alert a national fear of a permanent Catholic State. Feeling in parts of the country became anti-Catholic and did little good for dissenters in general. Catholic churches and Dissenting chapels became targets for mob violence and James was forced to abandon his throne.

The **Toleration Act** of 1689 gave much greater hope to the dissenters, though still debarred them from office. Over the following twenty years, a thousand congregations were established throughout the country. In 1691, Presbyterian and Independent ministers in London formed a United Brethren and in 1702, together with the Baptists, formed the three denominations into a short-lived **Body of Dissenting Ministers.** So strong was this new spirit of toleration that these privileges were soon even extended in practice to Catholics and Quakers. The Quakers who had actually gained in strength through persecution, soon became numerically one of the most powerful of the dissenting groups, highly respected though somewhat exclusive. However, their rigidity of discipline and forbidding of marriage to outsiders and relatives led to their rapid decline. Many joined other denominations, particularly the Methodists and the Unitarians, whilst others who had attained positions of more prominence in Society, embraced the Anglican Church. As the country settled into a state of comparative religious peace, so too did this mood give rise to a moral and religious re-awakening.

The Religious Revival

The revival had its roots perhaps in the Catholic policy of James II through which Englishmen saw more clearly what they were in danger of loosing. The theme between high church and dissent became the focal point of political and religious debate. It gave impetus to the work of a number of societies operating within the Church promoting Christian ideals in individuals and in families. It saw in the founding of dissenting schools at all levels, a challenge to provide charity schools throughout the country to educate the poor. A moral code based on Christian principles became in effect the way of life. During this period however, dissenting congregations declined substantially, many of its ministers having to petition for relief. Congregationalists began to take less interest in their church affairs whilst large numbers of Baptist congregations disappeared altogether. Disruption had been increased by a publication in 1716 supporting a scriptural doctrine of the Trinity. Those with Unitarian views, if supported by their congregations, became Unitarian. Those who disagreed, became either Congregational or reverted to the Anglican Church.

The revival did have lasting repercussions through the growth of religious societies and the desire to return to the simple teaching of Christ. In 1738, a small group of Moravians met in London. Based on Lutheran principles but with a form of Presbyterian administration, a movement emerged. Although making little headway amongst existing dissenters, Meetings were established in Derbyshire in 1740, and by

1743, in Yorkshire, Wiltshire and Lancashire. In 1736, Robert Sandeman, a student at Edinburgh, came under the influence of John Glass, whose views of justification by faith alone found support in a group at London in 1762, followed by other Sandemanian groups at Liverpool, Newcastle, Nottingham and Whitehaven, a few in Wales and some in New England. In 1753, Benjamin Ingham severed a long connection with the Moravians and formed a group based on Moravian principles but with Calvinist doctrine. Within two years there were fifty groups mostly in Yorkshire and Lancashire. Influenced by the Sandemanians in 1760, the movement later broke up into factions of other denominations. The remaining thirteen Inghamite groups merged with the Scottish Daleite group in 1814. Following the beliefs of Emanuel Swedenborg, a Unitarian who preached spirituality of salvation through a response to divine truth, two Societies were formed to publish his writings. The Manchester Society formed in 1782 and the London Theosophical Society formed in 1783, merged in 1807 to form the London Swedenborgian Society. In 1788, the first New Jerusalem Church was opened in London followed by others at Birmingham (1791), Manchester (1791), Liverpool (1793) and Accrington (1802). The movement spread through the midlands, the south west and the east and by 1851 there were some 50 registered chapels comprising congregations mainly from the poorer classes. Universalist views appear to have been fairly widespread in the eighteenth century, particularly amongst Unitarians but organised groups were not evident. In 1792 a group of Universal Dissenters was formed in Edinburgh and a few chapels under a Universalist banner were formed in the south west, but the only attempt at organisation appears to have stemmed through a magazine called the **Universalist** founded in 1850 and associated with David Thom, a former minister of the Liverpool Scotch Church who in 1825 had formed an independent Berean Universalist congregation. Under the leadership of Rev. J. Darby, whose pamphlet on the nature and church of Christ in 1828 aroused protest against the worldliness and clericalism of the Church, a group met for private worship. Other groups followed throughout the country during the next decade, taking the name of the Plymouth Brethren, from their group meeting at Plymouth. At the other end of the dissenting spectrum, the Presbyterian, Edward Irving with others, claimed the gifts of 'tongues and prophecy' and in 1832 formed a congregation in London. Although organised through twelve apostles and using Catholic ritual, the congregations of this 'Catholic Apostolic Church' were loose knit and were often comprised of regular members of other denominations. Six other groups developed in London and the movement spread to other parts of the country, to Germany, to Switzerland and to America.

Undoubtedly, the most important religious influence of the eighteenth century arose from the void created by the national Church, now so remote from its parishioners, that to some, it had become as moribund as the Catholic Church before the Reformation. The poorer classes felt neglected by a Church whose clergy thought more of clerical ambition, worldly life and pluralism than the care of souls. A small group led by John Wesley and his brother Charles, influenced to some extent by the Moravians, met to restore within the Church this lost spiritual holiness. Wesley, with one of his followers, George Whitefield, began open-air meetings from 1739, not without some harrassment, but nevertheless enabling an organisation of Societies and Classes to be established. Differences between the followers arose and Whitefield's Tabernacles maintaining a Calvinist doctrine of pre-destination and Wesleyan Preaching Houses stressing justification by faith, drifted apart. Wesleyanism then spread rapidly through itinerant revivalist preaching. In 1744, organised under an annual Conference, Circuits were established for the preachers which soon divided and sub divided into new Circuits as the movement grew. By 1747, the Calvinist Methodists had 31 Societies in England and Wales, but Whitefield's appointment as Chaplain to the Countess of Huntingdon led to uncertainty over lines of control. With a number of Connexion Meetings formed under the protection of Lady Huntingdon and Whitefield's chapels drifting into Congregationalism, breaks were inevitable. The Welsh brethren severed their connection with Whitefield and remained within the Church until 1811, becoming known as Welsh Presbyterians. The Calvinist Methodists formed their own independent group in 1763; the Connexion broke away from the Anglican Church in 1779 and by his act of ordaining a minister in 1784, Wesley effectively also broke away from the Church, although not agreeing to formal dissenting status until the closing years of the eighteenth century.

The Age of Industry

The birth of an industrialised society during this period was by no means a matter of chance. The very spirit which engendered the revival and which influenced the development of commerical education by those nonconformists excluded from the universities, played no little part in shaping this future. Early Puritans had included such families as Foley, Crowley and Hanbury which developed commercial interests in Staffordshire, Durham and South Wales. The Quakers provided such families as Darby, Huntsman, Lloyd and Reynolds to direct the iron and steel industry. The Baptist, Newcomen and the Presbyterian Watt, specialised in engineering. Independents like Roebuck and Dawson developed iron smelting, Unitarians, M'Connel and Greg, cotton spinning, and the Swedenborgian, Crompton, mining. Across the entire face of the country, it was the nonconformist who provided the leadership which enabled the industrialisation process to become so successful. This new commercial individualism developed into a national pride and toleration became less a matter for debate. After the dangers of two Jacobite rebellions had passed, in many parts of the country even Catholic worship was not hampered. New chapels were erected but it was still largely a movement of underground resistance. Only after the passing of the Catholic Relief Act in 1791, did Catholic parish life return to some state of normality. Even then, full civil equality was not obtained until the **Catholic Emancipation Act** of 1829. The fruits of the later Oxford Movement, developed by Cardinal Newman, a Catholic convert, stimulated this revival. The further influx of Irish and Italian workers and artisans and the simple piety of the Catholic clergy won many converts so that by 1850 the Catholic Church was ready to have its National Hierarchy restored.

By the beginning of the nineteenth century, this liberal influence had been replaced by an evangelical zeal, inspiring nonconformists with missionary work into the new industrial areas. Wesleyanism had already struck the chord of the nation gaining adherents in hundreds of thousands. By 1837 they could muster 341 Circuits in England and Wales, but symptomatic of the age, offshoots proliferated. A **Methodist New Connexion** sharing government between church and laity, was formed as early as 1797 and by 1837 had 30 circuits mainly in the north and in the midlands. A group of Quaker Methodists retaining ministerial control, operated from about 1806 under various names: **United Churches of Christ** in 1833, **United Free Gospel Church** in 1841 and **Independent Methodist** in 1898. **Bible Christians**, formed in 1815 by William O'Bryan, developed mainly in the south west and by 1837 had some forty two Circuits. Three other groups, resented the dominance of the Methodist Conference. **The Protestant Methodists** from 1827, the **Wesleyan Methodist Association** from 1836, joined by the former in 1837 and the **Wesleyan Methodist Reformers** from 1849, joined by the majority of the latter in 1857, formed the **United Methodist Free Churches**. With the further merger of the new Connexion and the Bible Christians in 1907, the group became known as the **United Methodist Church**. Those against union formed the **Weslayan**

Reform Union. From 1808, Hugh Bourne, who had been expelled from a Wesleyan Circuit for open camp meetings to the rural poor, found avid support for a new movement in the East Midlands. From 1812, under the banner of **Primitive Methodism**, the movement grew rapidly, spreading throughout the country and appealing most to those lower ranks of society which industrialisation in both town and country appeared to have left behind without identity. Persecution was rife, often affecting its supporters as much as its preachers but the movement's ability to provide a message of hope, sustained its development. By 1837 there were 150 Circuits in all parts save the south-east. In 1932, these, the Wesleyans and the United Methodist Church finally merged to form **the Methodist Church.**

The Baptist movement lost much of its support in the eighteenth century and continued to encourage factions. A strongly evangelical New Connexion was formed in 1770 and by about 1800 had some forty churches. Those with rigid Calvinist views broke from the Particular Baptists as Strict Baptists. They in turn split into various other groups usually known by the names of their journals: **The Gospel Heralds** from 1833; **The Gospel Standards** from 1835 and the **Earthen Vessels** from 1945. The Strict and Particular Baptists had formed a Union about 1812 and to the remnants of this, the General Baptists merged in 1891 as the Baptist Union, despite their feeling towards congregational autonomy. It is worth noting here that full membership and inclusion in the records of all the more exclusive sects was not normally available to the casual worshipper. The Congregationalists found much affinity with the Calvinist Methodists but soon also felt the need for voluntary association with its followers. Following the emergence of County Unions, a General Union of Independents was formed in 1806 merging later with the Home Missionary Society, all again merging as the Congregational Union in 1831. Unitarian principles developed more openly following the removal of laws against denial of the Trinity in 1813. In 1825, the British and Foreign Unitarian Association was formed, drawing heavily from other nonconformist groups as well as the Anglican Church. The decimation of the Presbyterian Church through this appeal, was partly offset by closer ties with the Scottish Church. In 1836, they joined with English congregations of the Scottish Church to form the **Presbyterian Church in England.** However, secessionist churches remained outside the Union and it was not until 1876 that they joined the English Presbyterians to form the **Presbyterian Church of England.** In 1972 this body merged with the Congregational Church to form the **United Reformed Church.**

PART TWO — GENERAL SOURCES AND REPOSITORIES

Nonconformist Registers

The earliest dissenting books recording baptisms appear to date from about 1642. Undoubtedly, baptisms and some marriages took place outside the Church well before this time but the risk of discovery for these illegal practices made record keeping inadvisable. Catholics were perhaps the only denomination to continue using their own clergy wherever possible throughout penal times but the majority of their early registers commence only from the eighteenth century. However it was not uncommon for Catholics to go through a second form of marriage and have their children baptised in the Anglican Church as an outward sign of compliance with the law.

Unlike other congregations, the Quakers had no clergy but recognised the need for securing legal status for themselves and their children. Although then under severe persecution they established in 1656, a system of record, parallel to that of the State which was reinforced in 1669. Their administrative hierarchy consisted of a **Preparatory Meeting** based on a single community, of which there were few before the middle of the eighteenth century, grouped into a **Monthly Meeting**, the principal meeting of the Society responsible for general affairs, including membership and marriage. These were grouped into County **Quarterly Meetings**, a form of pastoral court of appeal and these in turn formed the **Annual London Meeting**. Entries of births (not baptism), marriages and deaths mostly with places of burial, were the responsibility of the Monthly Meeting and details were often compiled from independent records of the individual congregations. In 1776 the system was overhauled. Birth-notes and burial notes were standardised and entered in the Monthly Meeting registers whilst duplicate entries on printed forms were kept by the Quarterly Meeting. Some of their early registers contain composite entries whilst others contain matters relating to the Society's affairs. Entries of births took the form similar to that for an Anglican baptistm but many of the earlier registers contain retrospective entries, some as far back as the sixteenth century. Quaker marriages took the form of an open declaration by both parties following an exhaustive investigation into their eligibility to marry. Marriage certificates often contain lists of relatives and friends who witnessed the occasion. Before the advent of their own burial grounds, Quaker death registers give the place of burial as the Anglican churchyard but there was also preferential use of orchards and gardens.

Many of the early records of the seventeenth century took the form of Church Books recording not only entries of births and baptisms but also matters relating to the affairs of that congregation. The establishment of civil registration in 1653 made separate records unnecessary and until 1662 many of the dissenting ministers, as clergy of the established Church, used their parish registers. Most of the surviving dissenting registers commence after this date but as there was no obligation for their upkeep large numbers were undoubtedly destroyed or simply lost. It would be foolish to imagine that every record of our nonconformist ancestors is contained solely in what has survived. Another problem for the historian arises from the habit of using one register for the entire area covered by that congregation. In some cases, the register, which was only the personal effect of the minister and not a legal document, was taken with him in a move to another location and continued there. One such Norfolk register recently came to light in Australia. The problem is more acute with Methodist registers which rarely start before the early 1790's. Rapid growth and subsequent contraction through an organisation of Circuits meant that ministerial responsibility for a given area was ever changing. The researcher needs to discover not only which villagers belonged to a particular Circuit throughout the period of these boundary changes but which Circuit register was in use for that particular area and time. Apart from those used by Quakers, dissenting registers followed much the same format as those of the Anglican Church but invariably drew their congregations from a much wider area of surrounding villages.

Entries of baptisms, which in the case of the Baptists relate to adult baptism, often include details of birth. Catholic and Huguenot baptisms have a special interest in that they often include details of godparents. Presbyterian registers tend to be somewhat more irregular though occasionally, the information given is more detailed. Methodist ministers tended to take their registers with them around the Circuit, whilst other denominations centred registration around their congregational building, though this practice cannot be taken as rigid. After the passing of **Hardwick's Act** in 1753, marriages outside the Established Church were forbidden. Undoubtedly, before this, most marriages took place in the parish church, though marriages in meeting houses and private chapels were by no means uncommon. Quakers became exempt under the Act and Catholics frequently continue to ignore its directions, although a private ceremony was often followed by another in the parish church. Baptists suffered most under the Act as clergy were reluctant to marry persons who had not been baptised. Not until 1836, were ministers allowed to obtain licences for marriages and even then, a civil registrar had to be present, an encumbrance not removed until 1898. Few congregations had their own burial grounds before the eighteenth century and with the exception of the Quakers, most burials took place in the parish churchyard. Many registers of deaths do however give additional details of burial outside the churchyard and in the case of Quakers, there was even a preference for their own orchards and gardens. In the early part of the nineteenth century, several more dissenting burial grounds were opened and these must form an important source for the historian.

In 1836, a commission, renewed in 1837, was established to enquire into the state, custody and authenticity of nonconformist registers with a view to seeking their deposit with the Registrar General. At first, there was some reluctance to deposit and generally, Catholics and Quakers refused to comply. Some congregations had not kept registers at all but had entered births, baptisms, marriages and deaths amongst their own records. However, once the benefits of deposit became more evident, many congregations deposited either their original registers or registers compiled from their other records for this purpose. Many chose to make a complete transcript before deposit and some care must be exercised to determine which is the original and which the copy. A catalogue of all registers deposited, arranged by county, was published by the Registrar General in 1841. These include some 1445 Quaker registers, 79 for Catholics, 194 for Presbyterians, 6 for Unitarians, 871 for most of the various Methodist denominations and registers for some 431 Baptist chapels and 1278 Congregational chapels. In 1857, a further commission with the same aims was set up. Despite continued refusal from the Catholics, a further 292 registers were received of which 25 were rejected and of which 121 came from the Quakers. In 1859, the Registrar General published a consolidated and more accurate list of deposits but despite attempts to correct previous mistakes, many errors remained. Invariably, start dates of registers were taken from the first entry of the first page and no attempt appears to have been made to differentiate between the various denominations which used the registers during their periods of religious mobility. A typical case might involve a register commenced by the Calvinist Methodists, continued by the Wesleyans but taken over and surrendered by the Countess of Huntingdon's Connexion in whose name it is listed.

By this time, the registry contained all known registers for Huguenot and Walloon Churches. In addition, the smaller Sects provided registers for 8 Catholic Apostolic Churches, 19 New Jerusalem Churches, 8 Inghamite Churches, 19 Moravian Churches and one Universalist Church. Quakers, to safeguard the loss of these registers, made digests in some 85 volumes, of 260,000 births, 40,000 marriages, and 310,000 deaths, all arranged under the initial letter of the surname. These are now in the Friends Library but copies of local entries were sent to local Meetings and may also be found in County Record Offices. However it should be remembered that these digests contain less information than the original entries now in the P.R.O. to which reference should be made. As interest expanded, large numbers of previously unknown registers were located from church or private sources and many of these have been deposited in Record Offices, particularly those of the Methodist Church. The Mormon Church have microfilms of most if not all of the registers at the P.R.O. and have extracted baptisms and marriages for incorporation into their International Genealogical Index, available on microfiche. However, the index is prone to error and care in its use is recommended. Transcription of surrendered dissenting registers is now carried out by family history societies on a fairly widespread scale and as a result, a large number of register publications have been added to those already published by other historical bodies.

Dr. Williams Library

The best known source for early nonconformity lies within the collection of books and manuscripts bequeathed to the public by an eminent Presbyterian, Dr. Daniel Williams which from 1729 was housed in the London Dissenters Library. Further accessions relating to individual congregations together with biographical indexes and copies of the publications of denominational and historical societies give this library a unique prominence. Now housed at 14 Gordon Square, London as Dr. Williams Library, there are useful indexes to the collection, listing under both subject and author and arranged both chronologically and topographically. The collection includes Evan's list of congregations compiled in 1772. During the course of its development, nonconformity suffered from a lack of legal status. This was most widely felt with the need to provide evidence of birth. In 1743, the Dissenting Deputies, representing Baptists, Independents and Presbyterians, established in the Dissenters Library, a register for the births of their children. The idea was successful enough for the College of Arms to make an unsuccessful imitation in 1748. The register became open to any parent regardless of creed or residence and willing to pay a fee of 6d. to register the birth of their children. For the family

17

historian, the information given is unusually detailed and included names of parents, the exact place and date of birth and the name of the maternal grandfather. Support was at first limited and by 1769 the register contained only 309 entries. Thereafter, ministers found it useful to use the library to deposit their register books. Registrations gradually increased and by 1837, 48,975 births had been registered. These records are now housed in the Public Record Office under Group RG.

The Public Record Office

Apart from nine thousand or so non-parochial registers, the registers of baptism (1742-1837) and original certificates (1742-1840) from Dr. Williams Library, the Record Office holds the registers of the **Metropolitan Wesleyan Registry** covering the period from 1808 to 1888. There are also burial registers for Bunhill Fields, the Dissenters burial ground in London and registers of marriage conducted by irregular clergy in the Fleet prison, the King's Bench prison, Mayfair and the Mint at Southwark covering the period from 1667 to 1754. Trust Deeds of nonconformist churches may often be rewarding for these list names of trustees and often, their replacements. The P.R.O. holds the trust deeds enrolled on the Close Rolls from 1736 with topographical bound indexes to 1870 and thereafter indexes on card. For general nonconformity, there are the Oath Rolls from 1779 to 1847 and Attorneys Oath Rolls from 1830 to 1875. For Catholics, records relate mainly to their persecution. The Recusant Rolls 1592-1691 contain a proportion of non-Catholic Dissenters but in the main, relate to the more prominent offenders. There are also various returns of Papists and their estates and lists of attorneys from 1790 to 1875. The returns for the 1851 religious census are also held here. A more detailed record of holdings can be found in the publication *Tracing your Ancestors in the Public Record Office* Cox & Padfield (1981).

Dissenting Registration

In addition to the record of registration of births afforded by the Dissenters Library, other forms of registration were in operation from the seventeenth century. Mention of the licenses issued in 1672 has already been made. These survive in Lambeth Palace Library and amongst the State Papers in the P.R.O. but have been listed by Turner. Registrations of Meeting Houses under the Toleration Act of 1689 are found at first more often in records of Quarter Sessions, but later, more applications were made direct to the Church. In 1811, registration became compulsory with penalties for breach. Catholics and Unitarians had been allowed to apply for licenses from 1791, though the latter, only through Quarter Sessions. In 1818, Wesleyans established a Metropolitan Registry for the births and baptisms of their children. Certificates giving parents names, witnesses to the births and details of the baptism, together with the original registers containing over 10,000 entries, are now housed in the P.R.O. In 1836, dissenting houses could obtain licences for marriages and in the same year there was a government *Return of all Dissenting Meeting Houses and Roman Catholic Chapels in England and Wales*. (Parliament Paper HC.433 XL 267). In 1851, a religious census for all places of worship, gathered information on dates of erection, capacity and numbers of church attendance. This is also held at the P.R.O.

Quarter Sessions

Documents used at the sessions are known as **Session Rolls** and contain registers for oaths of allegience, lists of dissenting meeting houses licences, indictments, petitions and recognizances. **Indictment Books** cover the judicial business and **Minute Books** record the proceedings of the sessions. **Order Books** record case judgements, have contemporary indexes and are easier to use but have less detail than the Rolls. They can contain presentments for non attendance at Church, indictments for recusancy, registration of meeting houses from 1689 which latter record, by the nineteenth century, had been reduced to a printed format, ecclesiastical returns of chapel registration under the 1811 Act and oaths of allegiance.

Anglican Registers

Some mention has been made of entries of marriages and burials in Anglican registers. This practice was by no means uniform and many clergy refused to make any entries or perform the actual ceremonies. With two Acts of Parliament in 1695 and in 1700, dissenters' births had to be reported to the clergy who were instructed to make entries in the parish registers. The Acts were largely ignored but many registers contain entries, often with some cryptic comment pertaining to the nonconformist belief. During the period when many of the established clergy were themselves dissenters, entries of baptism, marriage and burial may relate to parishioners sharing the belief of their ministers but this should not be taken as an indication that all parishioners were so inclined. Particularly during the eighteenth and nineteenth centuries, religious mobility was high and it was not uncommon to find parishioners

1661

Jan — 10 This day the Elders brought in the charge against Sister Thomison of Thompson widow for scandalous walking and being called to answer to the charge she told them that they charged her falsly, and being called more she turned her back and went out of the meeting, upon which the Church Ordered the Elders and what Brethren would to meet and consider what was to be done that soo they might put an end to it next meeting /

18 Also the Church Ordered Brother Streak to come next meeting and Brother Williams to give him notice of it /

25 The Elders and some Brethren did meet the 24 Instant & this day our Brother Streat and Sister Thompson not coming it was this day Ordered that both of them should come July: 9: to give an account of their & miscarriages and in the mean time any Brother or Sister to speak with them /

July — 2: Admitted Mrs Deboral Albertson widow —

2: Baptized — Samuell Williams son of John: & Elizabeth —

9: Baptized — Lydia: Wilcox Daugh of Roger & Francis —

9: This day the Church expected Sister Thompson to come & give an account of her Miscarriages but she being not in Townes we apprehended it was Ordered she should come on the 16 Instant and Brother William Turner was desired to give her Notice of it at Oakly if come home Mr Tuby and some other brethren to speak with her but not to hinder her from coming to the Church /

9 This meeting Brother Streat came in & did Confess that he was charged with, & it was accepted in part and an Admonition given him both to convince him further of his evill, and also to be a means to keep him from the like sin and he was desired when he found his heart more broken to come to express it to the Church /

16: This meeting after Exercise Sister Thompson was called to give an account of the Miscarriages she was charged with but she Justifying her selfe and Condemning the Church the Eldership with the Church did proceed to a withdrawing from the said Thompson Thompson widow as from a heathen and publican that soo she might be ashamed /

30 Baptized — Lydia: Eldridg Daugh of William & Lydia /

August: 6 This day was kept as a day of humiliation to humble our selves before the Lord for the sins of the Nation and also for our own sins /

Septr 17 Baptized — Isaac Preston son of Isaac & Hester
— William Harmer son of John & Mary
William Harmer son of William & Posis
John King son of Andrew & Hannah

29 Admitted — Mr Giles Wakeman
Thomas Doary
Mary Colman: wr of John Colman: Seaman

October 1 Baptized — Mary Wakeman
Rachell Wakeman   } Daughters of Giles & Susan
Sarah Wakeman
Posis Wakeman
Samuell Quilt son of Moris & Deborah

changing their religious allegience, not only between denominations, but often away from and back to the established Church. Religious belief was therefore often fluid and was as easily open to change as the ability of particular ministers to gain new adherents.

Monumental Inscriptions

Few congregations had their own burial ground before the eighteenth century and the majority commence well into the next century. Quakers in particular, disliked the use of memorials for their dead though a few grounds date from an early period. Nonconformists had long fought an unsuccessful battle for recognition of their right to churchyard burial and it was not until 1880 that this was fully approved by which time many of the urban yards had become closed. Dissenting burial grounds rarely commenced before the nineteenth century beyond those for individual congregations. A notable exception is that at Bunhill Fields in London where it is estimated that during the period from 1665 to 1852, there had been 120,000 interrments. However, the registers commence only from 1713, contained in 31 volumes and are now housed in the Public Record Office. Another exception is Ballast Hill Cemetery, Newcastle, where it is thought burials may have commenced as early as 1609, though the oldest surviving inscription dates 1707 and the registers commence in 1792. Many of the later burial registers will now be found in County Record Offices or still maintained by the Cemetery Superintendent. A few others found their way into the Public Record Office. As many of the surviving stones pre-date the registers, this can be a most rewarding source for the historian. In recent years much work has been done by Family History Societies throughout the country to record these monuments and where possible to publish their results.

Church Books

Early nonconformist records, particularly those of the Independent and Baptist churches often pre-date entries of baptism. Generally, these early books contain details of the day to day affairs of the congregation and minutes of their meetings. In the absence of separate registers, entries of births, baptisms or deaths appear as they arose in sequence to the proceedings of the congregation, though entries are also found grouped together. This use of the books as a composite record of the congregation provided the main reason for a reluctance to deposit them as registers in 1837. Moravian Church Books are particularly valuable, giving in effect, a roll of membership with dates of admission

An Account of the Societys on the Norwich Circuit 1803

Norwich.

John Davison Xr	w
Hannah Coleman	w
Ann Ulter	v
James Lamb	v
Jno Bensley	m
James Hill	v
John Life	m
Ann Jay	m
Mary Branchflow'r	m
Rebecca Davison	s
Eliz: Spring	s
Eliz: Davison	s
James Bates	m
Margeret Bensley	s
William Barker	s
	15

2d Class -

James Dunn adr	m
Eliz: Dunn	m
Ann Allaway	w
Mary Harrow'n	m
Mary Forster	w

Rehoboam Porter	m
George Dunn	m
Maria Buscham	m
John Dingle	m
Sarah Barney	m
Sarah Galley	
John Drake	m
James Turner	m
Enoch Pye	s
Joseph Bull	15

3d Class

James Bullard Xr	m
Mary Bullard	m
Thos Whiely	m
Mary Whiely	m
William Cook	m
Sarah Cook	m
Eliz: Hastings	w
Mary Ladley	s
James Richardson	m
John Meals	m
Mary Short	m

A page from the Wesleyan Methodist Class Lists for the Norwich Societies 1803.

22

and cessation. The more detailed Quaker Minute Books covering until 1896, a separate hierarchy of meetings for men and women usually contain such variety of activities as applications and admissions to membership, removal and re-admissions to membership, testimonials for deaths and disciplinary proceedings. Church Books form part of a collective deposit and are now found usually in denominational libraries, County Record Offices or in the custody of current ministers or elders.

Membership Rolls

Most of the Dissenting churches maintained some form of record of membership. The Moravian Church had a conscientious view of keeping records and in addition to annual membership lists few of which have survived, they maintained a Congregation or Church Book in which were listed the names of members and their children in order of admission, their married state, occupation, name of former denomination and date of cessation of membership. Other denominations, particularly Baptists and Independents recorded much of this information and gave further details of reasons for cessation of membership whether by death, by transfer or by removal. Despite their general attitude to keeping records, the Quakers paid little attention to membership rolls and despite internal attempts, little effort was made before 1837. Methodist Circuits did keep lists of membership but these tended to be merely lists of members, though some of the early lists of class members have also survived. Again, these records will be found amongst deposits in dissenting libraries, County Record Offices or still with current ministers.

John Ryland University Library of Manchester, Oxford Road, Manchester M13 9PP holds the official archives of the Methodist Church transferred from London in 1977. Whilst original registers have largely been passed to county record offices, there are some 150,000 books and manuscripts including minutes and manuscript journals of all Methodist Conferences. There is also a collection of some 40,000 books and manuscripts relating to Unitarian churches. Other denominational records are also represented and include a good collection of Christian Brethren material, a collection of local and national Moravian material, the Archives of the Lancashire Independent College and most of the library of the Northern Baptist College.

Typical page from a Baptist Church Membership Register 1823-40 showing list of members by date of baptism and subsequent individual history.

No.	Members Names	When Baptized	By Whom	When Received	Separated	Restored	Dismissed	Died
65	Samuel Ward	Oct. 12th 1823	Jones Smith	Oct. 12th 1823			March 6th 1840	
66	Simeon Bryant		By General Baptist	Dec. 7th 1823			July 30th 1831	
67	Lucy Machon		Jones Smith	Dec. 7th 1823			July 10th 1832	
68	Mary Bedson	May 9th 1824	Jones Smith	May 9th 1824			Dec. 10th 1832	
69	Ann Minister	May 10th 1824	Jones Smith	Oct. 11th 1824				June 14 1839
70	Robert Iver	Sept. 5th 1824	General Baptist	Oct. 5th 1820				May 4 1846
71	William George		General Baptist	Oct. 24 1825	Dec. 25 1827			
72	Elizah Brakeman	May 6th 1827	General Baptist	Oct. 24 1825	Jan. 29 1836			
73	Robert Bryant		Jones Smith	May 6 1827	Jan. 3 1831	July 25 1840	Oct. 10 1800	
74	Ann Heath		Jones Smith	May 27 1827			July 1 1807	
75	Robert Hodges	June 12 1828		June 27 1828				
76	Ann Huffen							April 2 1805
77	James Hubbard		Jones Smith	June 21 1829	Oct. 4 1800	Aug. 10 1820		
78	Samuel Barton		Jones Smith	Aug. 9 1829	Oct. 4 1800	Aug. 10 1820		
79	Mary Bulloum	Aug. 9th 1829		July 4 1830		Aug. 10 1820		April 23 1826
80	Mary Smith	July 4th 1830	Jones Smith				Oct. 29 1808	June 5 1858
81	Robert Barrett	May 22 1831	Jones Smith	May 22 1831				
82	William Jolly		Jones Smith	Jan. 2 1832	July 10 1802			
83	Martin Jolly		Jones Smith	Jan. 1 1832	Jan. 27 1800			Feb. 12 1812
84	William Barton	Aug. 5th 1832	Jones Smith	Aug. 6 1832	July 6 1805	Aug. 22 1853	July 11 1849	
85	James Mead		William Barton	May 15 1836				
86	Mary Mead	May 15th 1836	William Barton	Nov. 15 1836			July 1 1850	
87	Charlotte Sharpe	May 16th 1836	William Barton	July 24 1837				
88	Sarah Smith	July 23 1837	William Barton	Sept. 30 1838				
89	John Smith	Sept. 30 1838	William Barton	May 10 1800			Apl. 24 1860	
90	Joshua Shipton		J. W. Oakley	June 10 1800				Aug. 2 1857
91	Robert Foreman		J. W. Oakley	June 10 1800				Oct. 30 1853
92	Lucy Foreman	June 10 1800	J. W. Oakley	June 10 1800	Jan. 1 1857	July 31 1860		June 15 1855
93	John Bunnett	June 10 1800	J. W. Oakley	June 10 1800				
94	Samuel Barrie	June 10 1800	J. W. Oakley	June 10 1800				July 5 1841

PART THREE – DENOMINATIONAL SOURCES & REPOSITORIES

Roman Catholic

Few Catholic registers were deposited in 1837 and most remain with their clergy or in Diocesan archives. Some Catholic archivists have been appointed recently to collect Diocesan records into a central repository whilst a few Dioceses have opted for deposit at Record Offices. Before the restoration of the hierarchy in 1850, the country was administered through a number of Vicars Apostolic. Archives at Westminster contain the correspondence of these Vicars Apostolic, much other material from the sixteenth century, registers of missions and embassy chapels, diaries, account books and private papers. There is a particularly useful list of over 20,000 confirmations from the northern counties made in 1687. The archives of the Northern Vicariate are held by the Bishop of Leeds, the Bishop of Hexham and Newcastle and Liverpool Record Office. Those of the Midland Vicariate are at Birmingham and those of the Western Vicariate are held by the Bishop of Clifton. Much of the records of religious orders are still in foreign archives but the Jesuits have an archive at Farm Street, London and the Benedictines at Downside and at Ampleforth.

Confirmation Registers are perhaps the most common form of record beyond the registers and these are likely to be found fairly widely. Earlier records of penal times are more likely found under records of persecution in the Public Record Office and in records of Quarter Sessions. In 1705, Deputy Lieutenants were requested to furnish statistics of Papists and later that year the request was repeated to the ecclesiastical authorities. The House of Lords Library holds lists for a few counties whilst a few returns survive locally. Further returns were made in 1767 giving details of name, age, occupation and length of residence. Apart from the returns for Chester and Durham, the House of Lords holds only summaries, though many of the original returns survive in Diocesan Archives. Two other principal sources of record lie in the **Churchwardens Presentments** and **Act Books** of the established Church and in the often valuable material found in family papers now deposited in Record Offices. The Catholic Record Society has published valuable material on Catholic history since 1905 and many of their books are devoted to complete register transcriptions. 'Recusant History' has been published from 1951 and more recently, **English Catholic Ancestor** has been formed to encourage its members to research Catholic families. There are in addition, a large number of local Catholic historical societies, Catholic journals and a range of Diocesan magazines.

An 1759 die 25 Oct bzoi infantes ca
Ric et Edz Miles conjgbs cui nn Riccardus
imposttd e patrino Tho Molby matrina
Susan: Crow

An 1759 die 4 Nov: bzoi infules ex
Cornelio et Maria Murry conjbs cui im-
posttd e nn Margaritta patrino Joa:
Fury matrina Clementina Harrison

An 1759 die 11 Nov: bzoi infantes x
Gul: et Sara Hill ojbs cui impshd e nn
Petrus patrino Gul Loyel matrina Sara
Pooley.

An 1759 die 18 Nov bzoi infules x
Car: et Anna Brown ojbs cui impshd e
nn Carolus patrino Gul Coniss matrina Eliz: Baker.

An: 1759 die 29 Nov bzoi infules x
Car: et Eliz Smath ojbs cui impshd e nn
Jacobus patrino Gul: Armstrong matrina
Ann Crow.

An: 1759 die 11 Dec bzoi infules x Jac:
et Frnsisca Warner ojbus cui impshd e nn
Fransisca patr: Jo: Morton Mat: Eliz Leech

An early Catholic Register for 1759 showing in Latin, details of baptisms and names of godparents.

Quakers

Whilst most of the affairs of the Society of Friends will be found in the books of their various meetings, separate books were sometimes maintained to record such activities as disownments, death testimonials and records of sufferings. Quakers were also in the fore of educational reform and established their own Meeting Schools from the seventeenth century and private and public schools from the eighteenth century. Admission books for most of the latter are extant and some have been published, but detailed records of meetings and private schools are rare. **Friends House Library** at Euston Road, London N.W.1 is the mecca for the Quaker historian. Provincial records of meetings have been decentralised into Record Offices but the library holds records of the Annual Meetings, the Central Committees and all London Meetings. There are the original digests of births, marriages and deaths numbering some 610,000 entries and a storehouse of other books and manuscripts and microfilms of Quaker records in other repositories. There are copies of Quaker serials from 1701 and a typescript biographical collection with some 25,000 entries. The Friends issued a number of serials which are useful for including sources of biography and registration.

Piety Promoted 1701-1829 contains some biographies.

The Annual Monitor 1813-1920 contains obituaries and biographies. An index of some 20,000 names was published as 'Quaker Records' in 1894.

The Friend from 1843 includes announcements of marriage and death. Announcements of birth commence in 1850 and obituaries from 1894.

The British Friend 1843-1913 includes announcements of births, marriages and deaths from 1845.

Other Publications
Friends Quarterly Examiner from 1867
Journal of the Friends Historical Society from 1903
Bulletin of the Friends Historical Society of Philadelphia 1906-1923
Bulletin of the Friends Historical Association 1924-1961
Quaker History from 1962
Archives of the Society of Friends, Mortimer, (Amateur Historian 3. No. 2 1956-7)

Baptists

Records of early Baptists have suffered to some extent by their desire for complete autonomy without need of association. Consequently, records of a national nature are somewhat sparse. Decentralisation of records has also been adopted.

The **Angus Library,** Regent's Park, Oxford, holds the National Baptist Collection of Records which include Minute Books of individual congregations, Committees and Associations, District Association letters and papers of Stepney College, and a range of books and other manuscripts.

The **Baptist Union Church,** 4 Southampton Row, London, W.C.1, which formerly held the Baptist Union Library now at Oxford, has a range of books including the Baptist Year Books, and Dictionaries and Memoirs of Ministers from 1832 to date. The Baptist Historical Society may also prove of use to researchers and correspondence should be sent to this same address.

The **Bristol Baptist College,** Woodland Park, Bristol, holds archives of the Western Baptist Association and manuscripts of John Rylands and William Prynne. See also under John Ryland Library.

Publications

The Baptist Annual Register 1790-1802
The Baptist Magazine (Particular) 1809-1907
The New Baptist Magazine and Evangelical Repository 1825-1826
The New Baptist Miscellany 1827-1832
Account of the Proceedings of the Annual Sessions of the Baptist Church, 1836-1844
Manual of the Baptist Denomination, 1845-1859
The Baptist Handbook, 1861-1972
The Baptist Union Magazine 1892-1895
Church and Household from 1896
Transactions of the Baptist Historical Society 1908/9-1920
Publications of the Baptist Historical Society from 1909
The Baptist Quarterly from 1922/3
The Baptist Union Directory from 1973

Most of the above publications contain some information of ministers, or individual biographies and obituaries and the **Baptist Historical Society** maintains a list of obituaries compiled from most of these. There are of course a number of regional groupings of congregations outside the Union, each with some form of record and there are also some congregations which still maintain their complete independence.

Congregationalists

The Surman index of some 30,000 Congregational and Presbyterian biographies, and accounts of churches and ministers are held by Dr Williams Library. **The Congregational Library** at Farringdon Street London EC4, holds church rolls, various books and manuscripts, the collections of Thomas and Joshua Wilson and Rev. T.W. Davids and minute books of various congregations, committees and associations. The archives of the Congregational Historical Society are now held by the United Reformed Church Library which see below.

Publications
The London Christian Instructor 1818-1825
The Congregational Magazine 1826-1845
Home Missionary Magazine 1820-1840
Christian Witness 1844-1878
Congregational Year Book 1846 to date
Transactions of the Congregational Historical Society from 1901

Presbyterians
The United Reformed Church Historical Society Library at 86 Tavistock Place, London W.C.1, holds twenty registers for some of the Presbyterian churches in London, Cumberland, Lancashire and Northumberland. It also holds the Carruthers Indexes which contain material on early preachers, preachers and congregations and minutes and histories of individual congregations. The Surman index at Dr Williams Library contains details of large numbers of Presbyterian biographies and accounts of churches.

Publications
The Presbyterian Messenger, from 1844
Journal of the Presbyterian Historical Society, 1914 to date

Unitarians
Most of the Unitarian registers surrendered by 1859 were listed as Presbyterian and this highlights the difficulties encountered when researching these two denominations.
The Unitarian Library at Essex Street, London W.C.2, holds archives of some national and local organisations, title deeds, reports, year books and a miscellany of denominational publications.
Manchester College Library, Oxford, holds the Martineau and other archives and has a collection of general nonconformist publications. Reference should also be made to the fine collection at the **John Ryland Library**, Manchester.

Publications
The Unitarian Chronicle 1832-1833
The Unitarian Magazine 1834-1835
Transactions of the Unitarian Historical Society 1917 to date

Huguenots

Although most of the Huguenot communities were close-knit and maintained the French language, in some areas into the nineteenth century, their congregations became dissipated and absorbed into the Anglican community by about 1800.

The Huguenot Library, University College, Gower Street, London, W.1 is the joint library of the French Hospital and the Huguenot Society of London. It holds the Wagner collection of some 900 Huguenot pedigrees and abstracts of wills. There are thousands of books and periodicals and extensive transcripts of other manuscripts.

The **French Protestant Church** at Soho Square, London, holds the archives of several of the London churches.

The Huguenot Society of London has been a model society for demonstrating how the records of a particular group can be systematically published. Many issues give complete register transcriptions and some give complete listings from the archives of the Public Record Office, on Returns of Aliens, Denizations and Naturalizations and Oaths of Naturalization. The Society's **Proceedings** run from 1885 to date and its publications run from 1887 to date.

Moravians

Despite the Moravian tendency for avid record-keeping there has been no move towards centralisation and records tend to remain within the keeping of individual churches. Additional records to those described under general sources will include minute books, often in German, congregational diaries, minutes of the elders and a normal range of administrative papers.

The **Moravian Church House Archive** at Muswell Hill, London, holds the surviving archives of closed churches, various correspondence and copies of memoirs and minutes of the Provincial Synod. There is no national historical society but the **Moravian Historical Society** of Pennsylvania occasionally publishes articles on the British Church history. See also under John Ryland Library.

Methodists

Archivists have now been appointed for all Methodist areas and detail can be obtained from the Archivist at Oldham St. Manchester. A polic of decentralisation has ensured that original registers are now deposite with local record offices but the official Church Archives at the John Ryland Library, Manchester still number some 150,000 books an documents. **The Wesley Historical Society** holds manuscripts from some individual congregations and printed material for all the Methodist churches. The Record Office of the Wesleyan Union is at 123 Queen Street, Sheffield.

Publications

The Arminian Magazine 1778-1797
The Methodist New Connexion Magazine 1797-1907
The Methodist Magazine 1798-1821
The Primitive Methodist Magazine 1819-1932
The Wesleyan Methodist Magazine 1822-1932
The Wesleyan Protestant Methodist Magazine 1829-1834
The Bible Christian Magazine 1832-1907
The Watchman 1835-1863
The Wesleyan Association Magazine 1838-1857
The United Methodist Free Churches Magazine 1858-1891
The Methodist Recorder 1861 to date
The Free Methodist Manual 1877-1899
The Methodist Times 1885-1937
The Methodist Monthly 1892-1907
Proceedings of the Wesley Historical Society 1897 to date
The Primitive Methodist Leader 1905-1932
The United Methodist Magazine 1908-1932
Transactions of the Society of Cirplanologists 1961 to date

Swedenborgians
The Swedenborg Society 20/21 Bloomsbury Way, London W.C.1 holds the register copies of the New Jerusalem Churches, Conference minutes and other records of closed churches. In addition there is a fine collection of related printed books and manuscripts.
For reference see *The Swedenborg Society Past & Present* F.G. Griffith (1948).

Selected Works of Further Reference
Original Records of Nonconformity under Persecution and Independence, G.L. Turner, 3 vols (1911-1914). These include the Episcopal Returns of 1665, 1669 and 1676 and list the nonconformist licences issued in 1672.
Sources for Nonconformist Genealogy and Family History, D. Steel (1973)
National Index of Parish Registers, series: D. Steel (1968-1975), P. Palgrave-Moore (1976-1985)
Sources for Roman Catholic and Jewish Geneaology and Family History, Steel & Samuel (1974)
Records of the English Province of the Society of Jesus, H. Foley, 7 vols (1877-1884)

Bibliographical Dictionary of English Catholics 1534-1902, J. Gillow, 5 vols (1885-1903)

Old Catholic Missions, J.O. Payne (1889)

Archives of the Society of Friends, R.S. Mortimer (Amat. Hist. 3, No. 2. 1956-7)

My Ancestors were Quakers, Milligan & Thomas (Soc. of Gen. 1983)

History of the English General Baptists, A. Taylor, 2 vols. (1818)

A Condensed History of the General Baptists of the New Connexion, J.H. Wood (1847)

A Baptist Bibliography, W.T. Whitley, 2 vols (1916-1922, reptd. 1985)

Associated Records of the Particular Baptists in England, Wales & Ireland to 1660, ed. B.R. White (1971)

A Baptist Bibliography, E.C. Starr, 25 vols, (American Baptist Hist. Soc. 1947-1976)

My Ancestors were Baptist, G.R. Breed, (S. of Gen. 1983)

Bibliography of Local Congregational History, Surman (Cong. Hist. Soc. 1947)

The Archives of Congregationalism, A. Green, (Amat. Hist. 3, No. 5. 1957)

A Select Handlist for Students of Congregationalism, (Ts. Cong. Lib. 1965)

Presbyterian Church of England Records, J.T. Darling, (Archives 5, No. 25, 1961)

Lists of Foreign Protestants & Aliens Resident in England 1618-1688, W.D. Cooper, (Camden Soc. 82, 1862)

A History of the Huguenots of the Dispersion, R.L. Poole (1880)

Huguenot Pedigrees, C.E. Last, 2 vols. (1924-1928)

Genealogy in Methodist Repositories, Rev. T. Shaw, (Gen. Mag. 2 No. 5, 1952)

United Methodist Free Churches, C.A. Beckerlegge (1957)

United Methodist Ministers and their Circuits, C.A. Beckerlegge (1968)

Selected Works for Further Reading

English Religious Dissent, E.R. Routley (1960)

History of the Reformation, P. Hughes, 3 vols. (1954-1956)

Anglicans and Puritans, The Basis of their Opposition 1558-1640, J.F.H. New (1964)

The Great Rebellion 1642-1660, I. Roots (1960)

The Development of Religious Toleration in England, W.K. Jordan, 4 vols. (1932 1940)

Freedom after Ejection, A. Gordon (1917)

Religious Toleration in England 1787-1833, U. Henriques (1962)

History of the Catholic Church in England, J. Flanagan, 2 vols. (1857)

The Story of Quakerism, E. Vipont, (1954, revd. edn. 1960)

History of the English Baptists, A.C. Underwood (1947)

The Story of Congregationalism, E.R. Routley (1962)

Methodism and Society, S. Andrews (1971)

Student's History of Methodism, J.R. Gregory, 2 vols. (1911)

History of the Primitive Methodist Church, H.B. Kendall (1919)

The Presbyterian Movement, R.G. Usher, (Camden Soc. 3rd Ser. VIII 1905)

Unitarianism, W.G. Tarrant (1912)

History of the Moravian Church, E. Langton (1956)